A
Book of
Schizophrenic Poetry

A
Book of
Schizophrenic Poetry

By
Renee Malorey

ARPress
ILLUMINATING IDEAS.
EMPOWERING VOICES

ARPress
45 Dan Road Suite 36
Canton MA 02021

Hotline: 1(888) 821-0229
Fax: 1(508) 545-7580

Ordering Information:
Quantity Sales. Special discounts are available on quantity purchases by corporations, associations, and others. For details, contact the publisher at the address above.

Printed in the United States of America.

ISBN-13   Paperback   979-8-89389-711-1
               eBook   979-8-89389-712-8

Library of Congress Control Number: 2024922136

Table Of Contents

At Years End

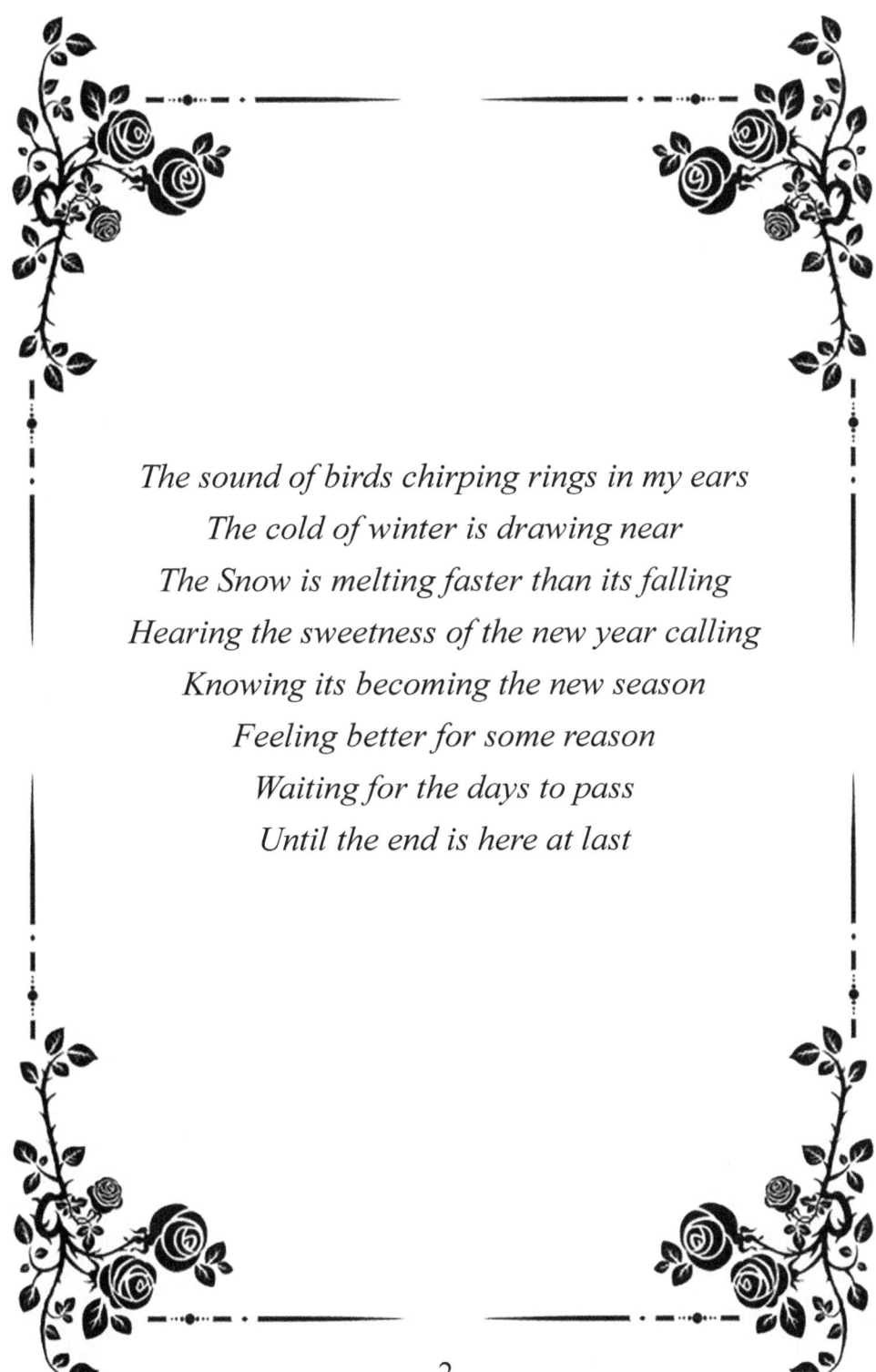

The sound of birds chirping rings in my ears
The cold of winter is drawing near
The Snow is melting faster than its falling
Hearing the sweetness of the new year calling
Knowing its becoming the new season
Feeling better for some reason
Waiting for the days to pass
Until the end is here at last

Autumn

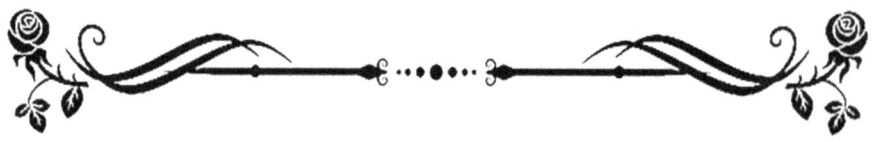

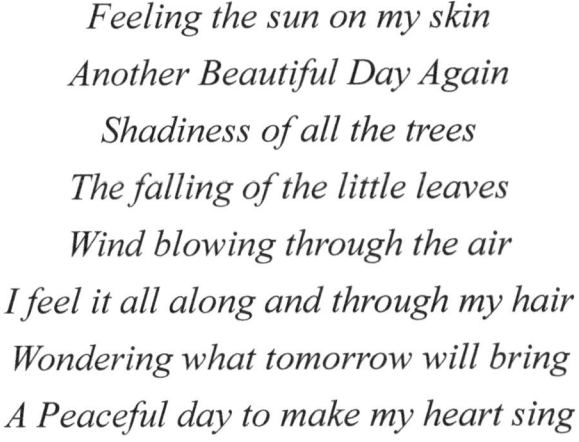

Feeling the sun on my skin
Another Beautiful Day Again
Shadiness of all the trees
The falling of the little leaves
Wind blowing through the air
I feel it all along and through my hair
Wondering what tomorrow will bring
A Peaceful day to make my heart sing

Butterfly Net

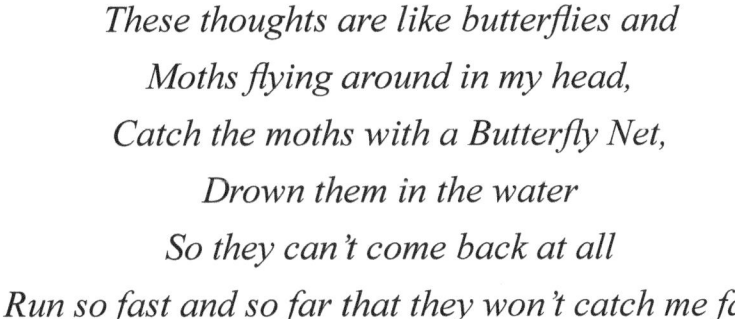

These thoughts are like butterflies and
Moths flying around in my head,
Catch the moths with a Butterfly Net,
Drown them in the water
So they can't come back at all
Run so fast and so far that they won't catch me fall.

Calculated Minds

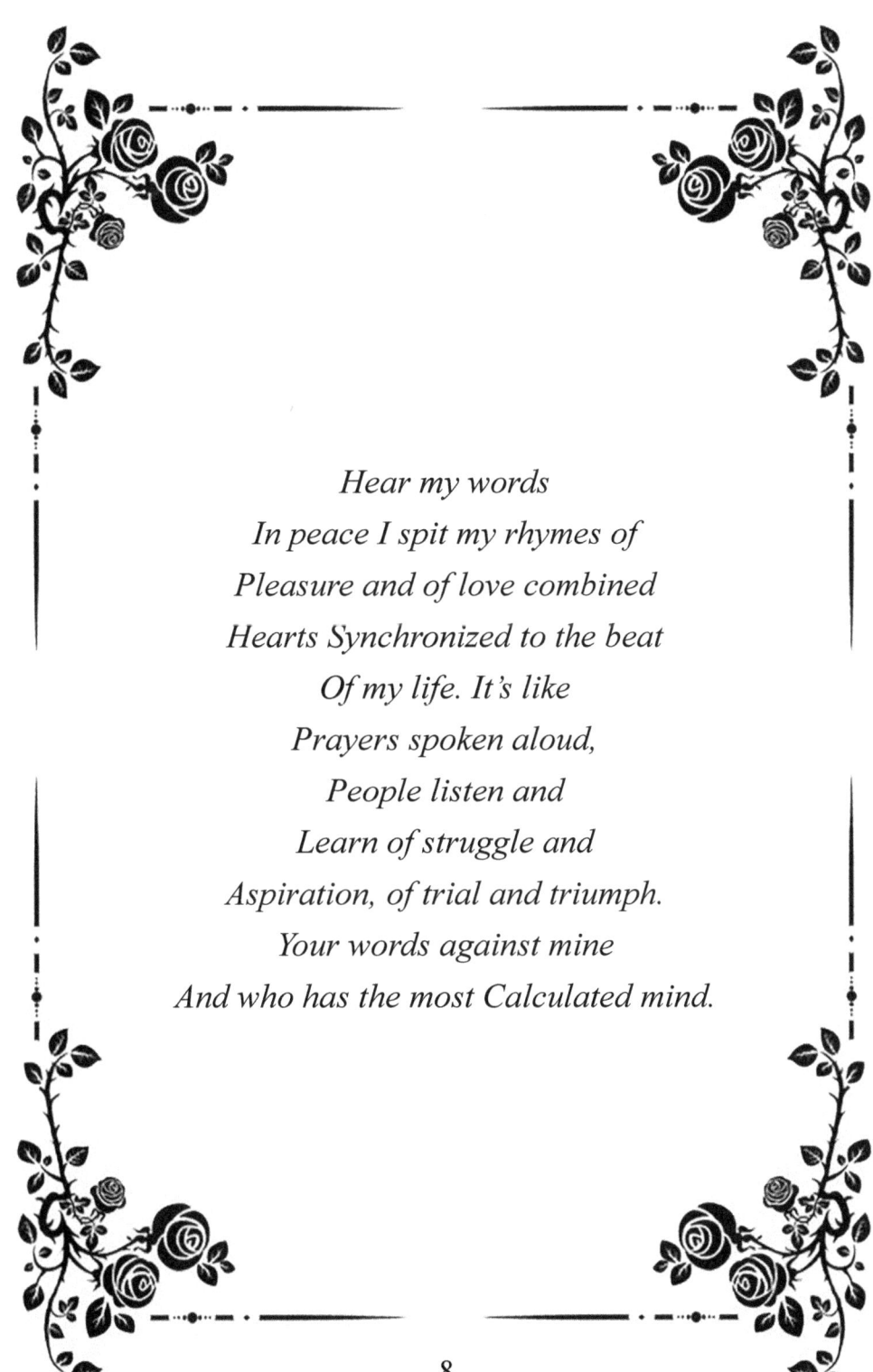

Hear my words
In peace I spit my rhymes of
Pleasure and of love combined
Hearts Synchronized to the beat
Of my life. It's like
Prayers spoken aloud,
People listen and
Learn of struggle and
Aspiration, of trial and triumph.
Your words against mine
And who has the most Calculated mind.

California

Downtown towers over me,
Yes I am in love with this city.
Now a speck in this vast world of ours,
Above the clouds like meteor showers.
Maybe in darkness it will call to us,
In light we will be Victorious
With Crimson Skies into the horizon.
Dozing off on a bed of grass beneath the Sun,
Until the day is done
Oh How I Never Want To Leave You!

Cherry Blossoms

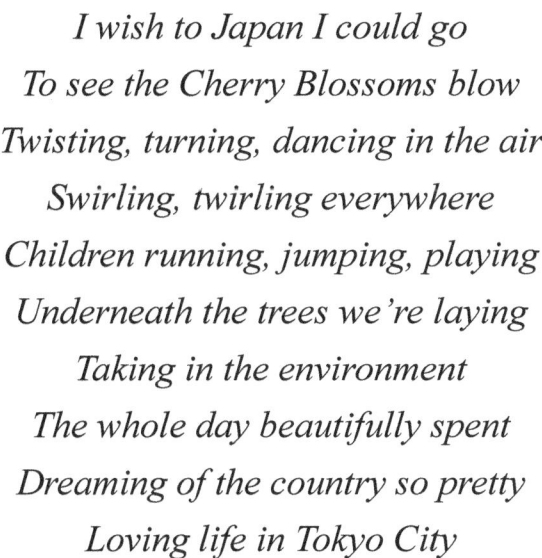

I wish to Japan I could go
To see the Cherry Blossoms blow
Twisting, turning, dancing in the air
Swirling, twirling everywhere
Children running, jumping, playing
Underneath the trees we're laying
Taking in the environment
The whole day beautifully spent
Dreaming of the country so pretty
Loving life in Tokyo City

Disappearance

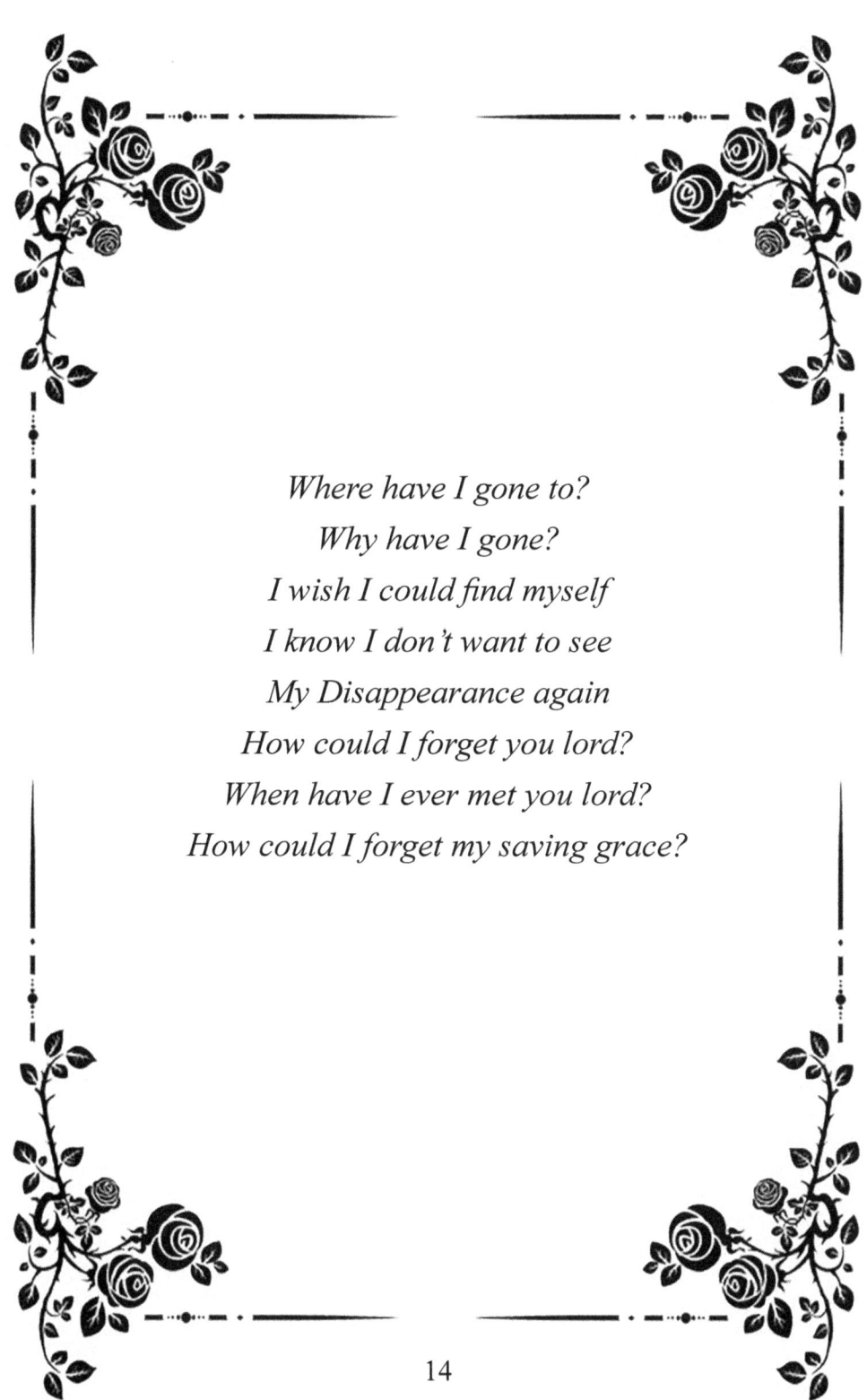

Where have I gone to?
Why have I gone?
I wish I could find myself
I know I don't want to see
My Disappearance again
How could I forget you lord?
When have I ever met you lord?
How could I forget my saving grace?

Freedom

Finding my freedom was hard
When I felt like I was doing it on my own
But finding my freedom now means
I don't have to do it all alone
I have people on my side
To hold me when I cry
To keep me walking on the path to light
Where once my path was all but filled with blight

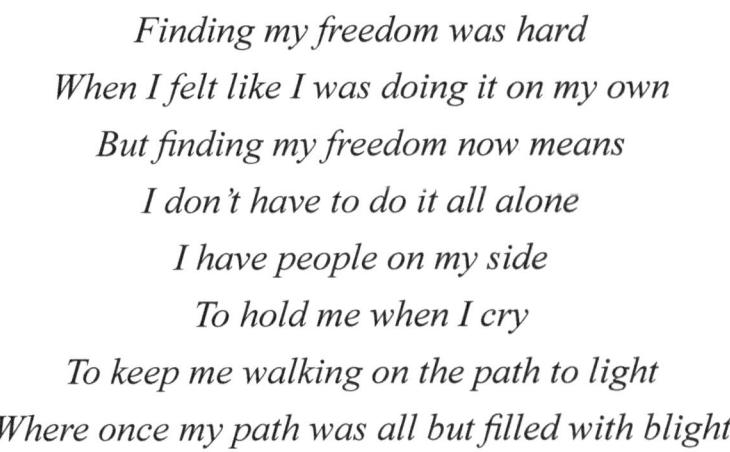

Growing

I'm stuck in this state of non-believability
Where I am me but I am not at the same time
Where I am not the only person in my mind
Now I wonder if I will grow old or no grow at all
Thinking about my life and the people in it
How they would feel in my position
How they would deal with my situation
I'm still growing and learning about
Me, Myself and I.
But the others in my head make me feel
As if I Myself am a lie.

Missing You

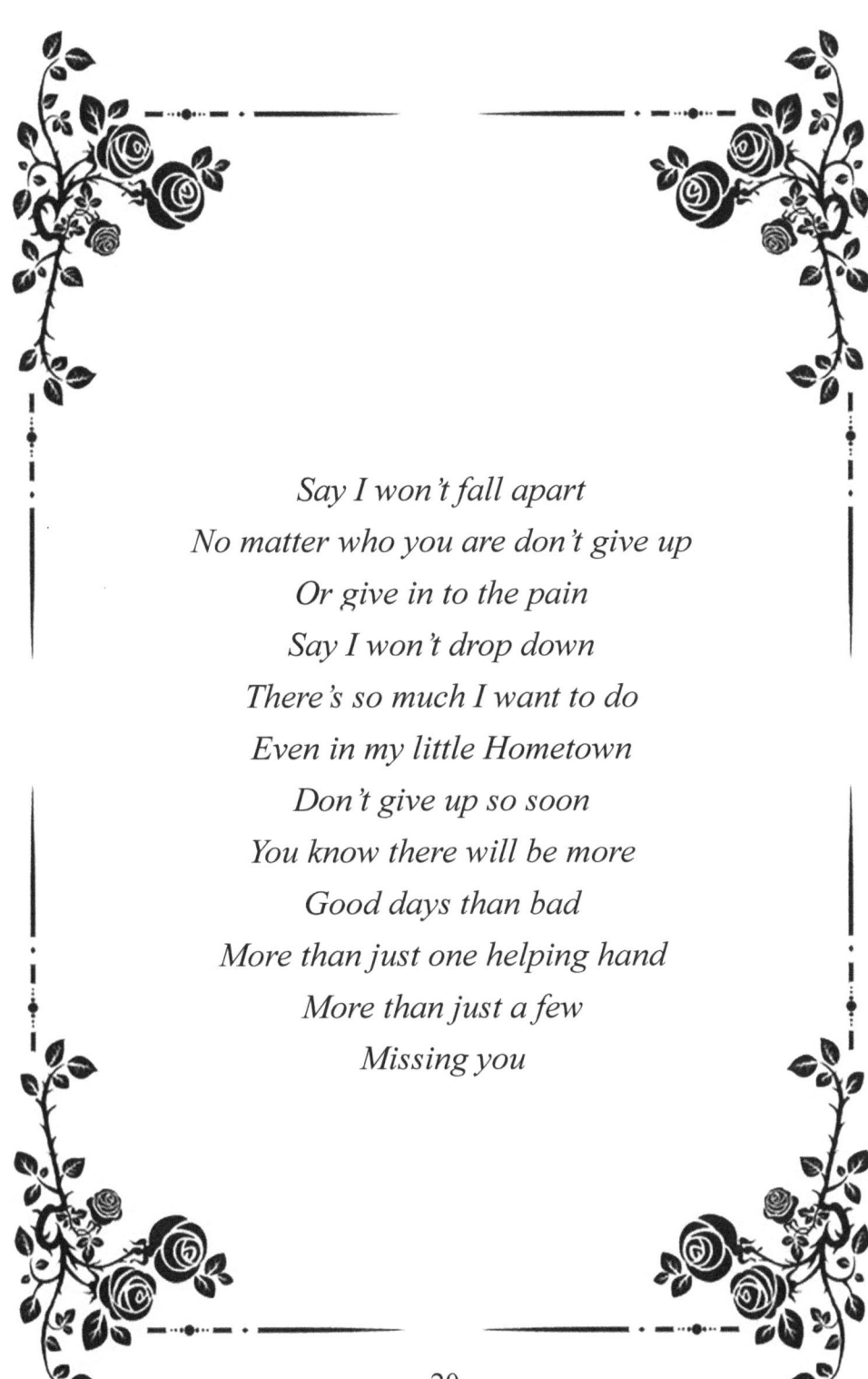

Say I won't fall apart
No matter who you are don't give up
Or give in to the pain
Say I won't drop down
There's so much I want to do
Even in my little Hometown
Don't give up so soon
You know there will be more
Good days than bad
More than just one helping hand
More than just a few
Missing you

Thoughts

My Mind is not my own right now
There are too many within
My mind is not my own right now
And some don't like my skin
I wish that I could get to me
To who I was before
I just want to be myself again
Get back to me once more

22

Unknown

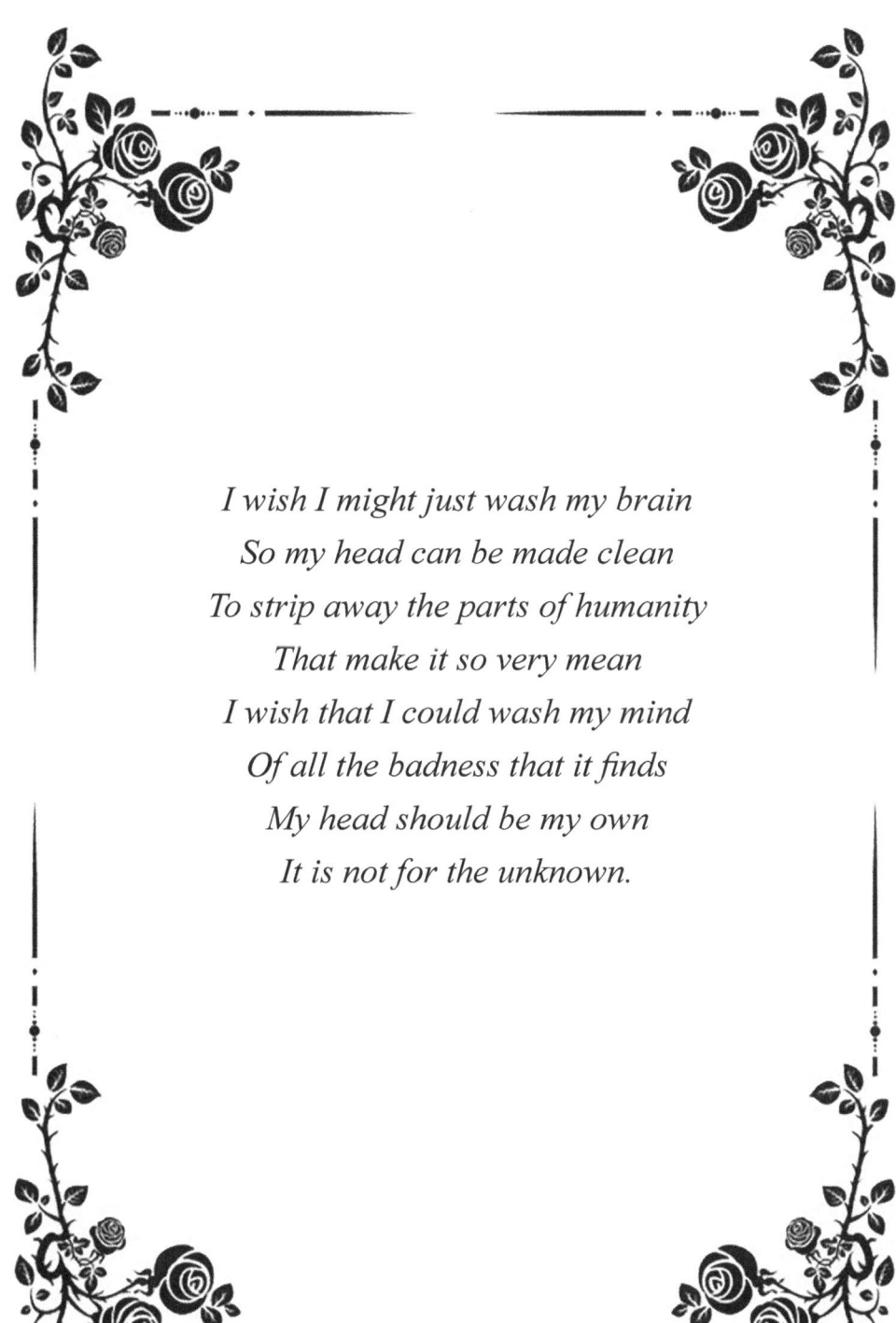

I wish I might just wash my brain
So my head can be made clean
To strip away the parts of humanity
That make it so very mean
I wish that I could wash my mind
Of all the badness that it finds
My head should be my own
It is not for the unknown.